YOUR KNOWLEDGE HAS

Andreas Bachmaier

Implementing iOS-Apps with iCloud Support

GRIN Verlag

Bibliografische Information der Deutschen Nationalbibliothek:

Die Deutsche Bibliothek verzeichnet diese Publikation in der Deutschen National-
bibliografie; detaillierte bibliografische Daten sind im Internet über http://dnb.d-
nb.de/ abrufbar.

Imprint:

Copyright © 2013 GRIN Verlag GmbH
Druck und Bindung: Books on Demand GmbH, Norderstedt Germany
ISBN: 978-3-656-38271-3

This book at GRIN:

http://www.grin.com/en/e-book/210118/implementing-ios-apps-with-icloud-support

GRIN - Your knowledge has value

Der GRIN Verlag publiziert seit 1998 wissenschaftliche Arbeiten von Studenten, Hochschullehrern und anderen Akademikern als eBook und gedrucktes Buch. Die Verlagswebsite www.grin.com ist die ideale Plattform zur Veröffentlichung von Hausarbeiten, Abschlussarbeiten, wissenschaftlichen Aufsätzen, Dissertationen und Fachbüchern.

BACHELOR'S PAPER

Degree Program ICSS

Implementing iOS Applications with iCloud Support

By: Ing. Andreas Bachmaier

Vienna, 23. Januar 2013

FACHHOCHSCHULE
TECHNIKUM WIEN

Kurzfassung

Information ist heutzutage für uns ein wichtiges Gut, sowohl im beruflichen wie auch im privaten Umfeld. Das Handy ist unser ständiger Begleiter und Tablets erfreuen sich, aufgrund der leichteren Bedienbarkeit (Displaygröße, größere virtuelle Tastatur), immer größerer Beliebtheit. Neben diesen mobilen Geräten besitzen viele Nutzer dann vielleicht noch ein Notebook oder einen Desktop-Computer. Viele Anwendungen (Apps) verwenden die Cloud um die Daten auf den unterschiedlichen Geräten synchron zu halten. Apples Lösung für die Cloud ist aktuell iCloud.

In meiner Bachelor-Arbeit werde ich zeigen, wie man Apps für iOS-Geräte (wie iPhone und iPad) entwickelt, die ihre Daten in der iCloud speichern. Nach einer Einführung in die Funktionen der iCloud, werden die Grundlagen der Datenspeicherung auf iOS-Geräten, anhand einiger Beispiele erläutert. Darauf aufbauend wird gezeigt wie die Daten in der iCloud gespeichert und auf andere Geräte synchronisiert werden können.

Schlagwörter: iPhone, iPad, iCloud, Daten-Synchronisation

Abstract

Nowadays Information is an important asset for us in the professional, but also private life. The mobile phone is our constant companion and tablets gain more and more popularity because of the ease of use (screen size, larger virtual keyboard).. In addition to these mobile devices a lot of users maybe also own a laptop or a desktop computer. Many applications (apps) are using the cloud to synchronize the data on different devices. Apple's solution for the cloud service is currently iCloud.

In my paper, I will show how to develop applications for iOS devices (such as iPhone and iPad) that store the data in the iCloud. After an introduction to the features of iCloud, I will describe the fundamentals of the data storages on iOS devices by giving several examples. The last chapter extends the application with integrating the three kinds of iCloud storages. Those types are based on and similar to local storages types.

Keywords: iPhone, iPad, iCloud, data synchronization

Contents

1 Introduction

The increasing proliferation of mobile devices and personal computers and the need to have all the personal or business information up to date means that data synchronization has to be as simple as possible. All big operating system vendors offer their own cloud solution, for instance Microsoft (Azure [1], SkyDrive [2]), Google (Google Drive [3]), Ubuntu (Ubuntu One [4]), and Apple (iCloud [5]). Each of those solutions works best with their own operating system, but could have some disadvantages, for instance missing features, on the other OS.

This paper uses the Apple environment and shows how you can build applications for iPhone or iPad, which save data into Apple's cloud solution iCloud. The start of this paper provides an overview of cloud computing and iCloud, afterwords you will see the iCloud from the user view and the developer view. Before we can write iCloud applications, we have to know how data can be saved on the device, starting from simple key/value pairs, like user settings, to documents and databases. With this knowledge the application can be extended to save data to the iCloud. In this paper I will develop a simple location based application to demonstrate all of those possibilities of data storage on the device or in the iCloud. The last chapter shows how data can be exchanged without using the iCloud.

1.1 What is Cloud Computing?

Cloud Computing isn't a new idea, but nowadays everybody is talking about the cloud. The main reason for the customer to use the cloud is, it makes it easy to exchange and synchronize the data of applications to all devices. John McCarthy already had already 1961 the vision of the future of time-sharing technology.[6]

"Cloud computing is a model for enabling ubiquitous, convenient, on-demand network access to a shared pool of configurable computing resources".[7] Those resources can be for instance servers, applications or storage. The NIST (National Institute of Standards and Technology) standard also describes different Service Models: Software as Service, Platform as a Service and Infrastructure as a Service.

Software as a Service (SaaS) means the application is running on the hardware of the provider and the consumer can use this services with a thin client, like a web browser, but also business applications. Typical SaaS applications are Facebook, Youtube, Google Apps. The main idea of Platform as a Service (PaaS) is to provide to the costumer a development framework or operating system, for instance Microsoft Azure. In the Infrastructure as a Service (IaaS) model the consumer can use the infrastructure of the provider, like storage, computation, networks and other computer resources.

Figure 1.1 shows an overview of those three service models and some example existing applications. You will find more detailed description about Cloud Computing here: [7] & [8]

1.2 iCloud Overview

Apple introduced iCloud on June 2011 as replacement of MobileMe. MobileMe was a fee-based cloud-service and included contacts, calendar, mail services, but also a storage solution

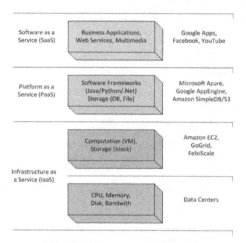

Figure 1.1: Cloud services [8]

(iDisk). iCloud isn't just a substitute, but an extension of the old service and includes some new features and application programming interfaces (API) for developers to build their own applications with integrated iCloud storage and data synchronization.

Now, iCloud is a free service - only some additionally features, like more storage, are fee-based. Apple describes iCloud on their homepage with the slogan "It's the easiest way to manage your content. Because you don't have to."[5] iCloud stores the user data, such as emails, photos, music, books, notes, documents in the cloud. In this case the cloud means many big data centres of Apple. You will find a complete list of the iCloud features on Apple's homepage.[5] In addition to those Apple applications there are a lot of third party apps, which use the iCloud to store and synchronize their data. This paper provides the knowledge, how to develop this kind of application and shows how the data can be saved.

iCloud is fully integrated on mobile devices - these are iPhone, iPad and iPod touch - and desktop devices - all desktop Macs and MacBooks, running on OS X Lion or higher. The Apple TV and Computers with the Windows operating system also can use parts of the iCloud, like photos, music, emails. The main features of iCloud are also available via web browser.[9] According to the NIST standard of Cloud Computing iCloud is mainly a SaaS model, but in parts also a IaaS model.

Figure 1.2: iCloud features [5]

2 iCloud

2.1 Users view of iCloud

To use iCloud the user has to setup the iOS device with an Apple ID. Many of the iCloud features are also integrated on Apple's desktop operating system OS X, or will be integrated in upcoming versions.

After activating the iCloud the user can choose in the settings windows for any supported application, if the data will be saved in the iCloud or not. This settings for the apps developed by Apple are summarized in a iCloud page, for all other third party apps, there is a separate settings page with the name of the application. The data, which is saved in the iCloud, is automatically downloaded if needed to all registered devices and is also available, when the device does not have an Internet connection. Changed data will be uploaded once the connection is re-established. Normally, there are no other manual operations to do by the user, only if there exists different versions of the document. This problem arises, when the changed data cannot be uploaded to or downloaded from the iCloud immediately. Your application has to handle this synchronization conflict, for instance by asking the user which version should be saved.

iCloud is especially designed for Apple devices and operating systems, but there also exist a control panel for Microsoft Windows. With this control panel it is possible to synchronize the contacts, calendar entries, mails, notes and photos, but there are much more features, which cannot be used by the windows version of iCloud.

The main features of iCloud are also accessible via web browser from any, also on not supported operating systems [9].

Figure 2.1: iCloud web page [9]

2.2 Developers view of iCloud

The vision of Apple for iCloud is a very simple and user friendly way to use it. But this means that the user doesn't know or see how the data are organized and stored on the device and in the cloud. It doesn't matter, there is no reason for the user to know that. As developer it is indispensable to know the internals of the iCloud storage.

There are three different types of iCloud storage: Key-Value storage, Documents storage and Database storage. Each of them is described in chapter 5 and are similar to the associated local storage types, described in chapter 4. In fact, the local storage and cloud storage uses many of the same mechanism and also the same classes.

As additional service Apple provides also an iCloud Developer web page. On this web page you can browse through the documents, which are saved in the iCloud. You will find your documents, databases and property list files, for applications, winch uses the iCloud document storage.

Figure 2.2: iCloud Developer web page [10]

iCloud is one of the major features of iOS 5 and the users, who are using this feature are growing every day. But not all devices are supporting this version of iOS. If you plan to purchase your application on iPhone 3G or older, make sure your application checks if iCloud is supported or not.

2.2.1 Testing & Debugging

For testing your iCloud solution you need a real device. The simulator doesn't support iCloud (yet). The first step to deploy the application on the device or in the AppStore is to create a provisioning profile and an AppID with activated iCloud feature on Apple's developer web page. Then you have to set in your Xcode project the entitlements for the target and enable iCloud for the Key-Value Storage and/or the Ubiquity Containers. A Ubiquity Container is the storage for the iCloud documents and databases on your device.

However, for debugging of all the iCloud features in your application it might be useful to have a second device to test the synchronization and conflict handling. For provoking version conflicts turn on the flight modus on one device, change some data on two devices. After you deactivated the flight modus check if your handling works as you have designed for your application.

Moreover, you also have to be patient, because the iCloud synchronization needs some time. Sometimes it is not easy to find out whether the application has an error or there exists other inconsistency in your ubiquity container on the basis of unresolved conflicts or changed document types.

3 Comparison iCloud with other Cloud Services

Besides iCloud there also exist many other cloud solutions with an API for iOS. Why should you use iCloud instead for example Dropbox? The main reason pro iCloud is the full integration in Apple's mobile devices with iOS. During the first setup of a new device such as iPhone or iPad the user is asked if he wants to use the iCloud. The easy setup and usage of iCloud results in more than 150 million iCloud user accounts (April 2012) [11]

Nevertheless, there is a point that speaks against iCloud. The integration in other operating system doesn't exist. If you need this integration, you cannot use iCloud and you have to use an other cloud solution instead or additionally. The table 3.1 shows a comparison of some frequently used cloud solution, which provides an API for iOS. On the developer websites you will find the API for iOS including the documentation and some example source code.

Features	iCloud	FTP WebDAV	DropBox	SkyDrive	Google Drive
mobile OS support	iOS	all	iOS Android	iOS Android Windows Phone	iOS Android
Server	Apple	self hosted or web space	Dropbox	Microsoft	Google
Free Storage	5 GB	—	2 GB	7 GB	5 GB
Office Integration	Apple iWork	—	—	Microsoft Office	Google Docs
File Sharing	readonly with URL	yes	yes	yes	yes
Minimum iOS version	iOS 5	iOS 2	iOS 4.2	iOS 4.3	iOS 3

Table 3.1: Cloud API Comparison

Instead of using a cloud solution you can use the old, but frequently used standards for file transfer through the internet: FTP and WebDAV. But this means you have to offer a server with those protocols or let the user configure their own server in your application. Many popular applications such as GoodReader have implemented almost all major cloud systems in their applications.

If you plan to use an other cloud solution in your application, you also should think about adding iCloud support, because the integration for this support doesn't mean much additional work when using the right components of the iOS frameworks.

4 Saving data on the device

Applications have to store various kinds of data, beginning from simple user settings until documents and databases. Those data can be stored on the device or in the cloud. This chapter describes the basics, how to store data on the device and what is necessary for understanding the iCloud storage methods.

4.1 Property Lists

Many applications need some preferences, for instance default values or some user specific settings. In iOS you can use the class NSUserDefaults to store your preferences on the device. NSUserDefaults allows only scalar values like boolean, integer, float or double and the following data types:

```
NSData, NSString, NSNumber, NSDate, NSArray, NSDictionary
```

Abstract type	XML element	Class
array	<array>	NSArray
dictionary	<dictionary>	NSDictionary
string	<string>	<NSString>
data	<data>	NSData
date	<date>	NSDate
integer	<integer>	NSNumber (intValue)
float	<float>	NSNumber (floatValue)
Boolean	<true/> or <false/>	NSNumber (boolValue == YES or NO)

Table 4.1: Property list types and their representations [12]

Those types are the standard property list object types. Property lists save the data with a name and a list of values. Each of the property list can include different object types. This means you can save a text with NSString and a array of numbers with NSArray, and so on. Property lists are serializable and deserializable, so it is possible to store the list on the file system in XML notation. The conversion from an object to XML and back is very efficient for small pieces of data. In most cases there is no need to save the property list directly to a file in your application. The main usage is to save them in the user defaults with the NSUserDefaults class.

Apple advises to use property lists for data not much more than a few hundred kilobytes [12] (Data Management - Property List Programming Guide - About Property Lists). If your application saves those settings to the iCloud, you have to note the key-value storage of the iCloud is also limited, see section 5.1 on page 23.

Property lists are also used in Xcode for the metadata of your application. Other, more complex, object types have to implement the NSCoding protocol, so the archiver can encode and decode the data. After encoding with an archiver this data can be stored as user defaults.

4.1.1 NSUserDefaults

Loading the user defaults data is very simple. You only need an instance of the NSUserDefaults, then you can access to every item in the property list with its name and object type. The following listing shows how to load a boolean value into to the property iCloud, which is a boolean value. The NSLog command is only to demonstrate if this loading works.

```
- (void)loadUserDefaults
{
    NSUserDefaults *userDefaults = [NSUserDefaults standardUserDefaults];
    self.iCloud = [userDefaults boolForKey:@"iCloud"];
    NSLog(@"iCloud: %s", self.iCloud ? "YES" : "NO");
}
```

Listing 4.1: Load UserDefaults

But what about saving the user default data? It's also very easy to implement.

```
- (void)saveUserDefaults
{
    NSUserDefaults *userDefaults = [NSUserDefaults standardUserDefaults];
    [userDefaults setBool:self.iCloud forKey:@"iCloud"];
    [userDefaults synchronize];
}
```

Listing 4.2: Save UserDefaults

You only have to set the value and its key name into an instance of NSUserDefaults. Depending on the property list type of the object, there exists several methods for setting or getting the data, for example: boolForKey or setBool, stringForKey / setString. iOS automatically stores those values to the disk by calling the synchronize message, but you also can send this message to store the data immediately. This is necessary for instance if your application is closing and you want save the latest changes. Figure 4.1 shows the user defaults property list, which is used in the listings 4.1 and 4.2.

4.1.2 Settings Bundle

Those messages load and save data without any graphical user interface and you can use these messages in any part of your application. However, if you want to give the user a settings window in your application, you need a settings bundle in your Xcode project. The settings bundle is a property list file. In this plist file you can configure one or more items as text field, slider or toggle switch. Xcode helps you to configure this property list. The settings page will be automatically created when the application is installed.

Key	Type	Value
▼ iPhone Settings Schema	Dictionary	(2 items)
▼ PreferenceSpecifiers	Array	(1 item)
▼ Item 0 (Toggle Switch – use	Dictionary	(4 items)
Type	String	PSToggleSwitchSpecifier
Title	String	use iCloud
Key	String	iCloud
DefaultValue	Boolean	NO
StringsTable	String	Root

Figure 4.1: Settings Bundle

The settings window looks like figure 4.2 on an iPhone. You should use this mechanism only for settings which are normally not often changed by the user, because it isn't very comfortable for the user to leave the application and go to the settings window.

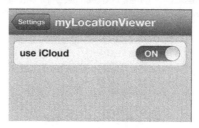

Figure 4.2: Settings Window

After changing the user defaults in the settings window, your application is starting with the actual values after executing the loadUserDefaults message. But what happens if your application is currently started and in the background? The next time you send this message you have to changed values. To inform about changes you have to implement an observer for NSUserDefaultsDidChangeNotification. A good place for this observer is didFinishLaunching-WithOptions message in your AppDelegate class or in viewDidLoad of your view controller class. The selector defaultsChanged is a method, in which you can update your user defaults in the application.

```
[[ NSNotificationCenter defaultCenter] addObserver: self
    selector: @selector( defaultsChanged :)
    name: NSUserDefaultsDidChangeNotification
    object: nil ];
```

Listing 4.3: NSUserDefaultsDidChangeNotification

The user default values, either used in the settings bundle or only in your code is also saved in a plist file in your application file system (more about the file system in section 4.2.1. You can use the iOS Simulator to look inside this file. Start your application in the simulator. Then you'll find the file in the folder: *~/Library/Application Support/iPhone Simulator/[iOS-Version]/Applications/[appGUID]/Library/Preferences/* In this file you see the keys you have used in the application and the saved values.

```
<?xml version="1.0" encoding="UTF-8"?>
<!DOCTYPE plist PUBLIC "-//Apple//DTD PLIST 1.0//EN" "http://www.apple.com/
    DTDs/ PropertyList -1.0.dtd ">
<plist version="1.0">
<dict>
  <key>Last Location </key>
  <data>
  YnBsaXN0MDDUAQIDBAUIHR5UJHRvcFgkb2JqZWN0c1gkdmVyc2lvbkkkYXJjaGl2ZXLR
  b25UaXRsZV8QFkxhc3RMb2NhdGlvbkNvb3JkaW5hdGVfEBRMYXN0TG9jYXRpb25UdWJ0=
  </data>
  <key>iCloud </key>
  <true/>
</dict>
</plist>
```

Listing 4.4: myapplication.plist

4.1.3 Archiving Objects

What about any other objects, which are not a property list? If you want to store those objects, you need a serialized representation of them. There are two ways to generate this serialized representation: archives and serializations. Both variants create an architecture-independent stream, which can be written to the file system. The difference is that archives provide more detailed information, for instance naming values. Archives can store Objective-C objects, but also Java objects. [12] (File Management - Archives and Serialization Programming Guide)

A coder object is needed to encode and decode the object data into/from a byte stream. This stream can be stored on the file system or in the property list. Stored byte streams can be decoded into an object. Those objects have to implement the NSCoding protocol, which requires two messages: "Initializing with a Coder" and "Encoding with a Coder".

The initWithCoder message decodes the serialized data into an instance of an object.

```
- (id)initWithCoder:(NSCoder *)decoder
{
    self.title = [decoder decodeObjectForKey:@"LastLocation Title"];
    self.subtitle = [decoder decodeObjectForKey:@"LastLocation Subtitle"];
    return self;
}
```

Listing 4.5: Initializing with a Coder

The encodeWithCoder message generates the serialized representation of an object.

```
- (void)encodeWithCoder:(NSCoder *)encoder
{
    [encoder encodeObject:self.title forKey:@"LastLocation Title"];
    [encoder encodeObject:self.subtitle forKey:@"LastLocation Subtitle"];
}
```

Listing 4.6: Encoding with a Coder

There exist several methods for encoding / decoding the data, depending on the object type, for instance encodeObject, encodeFloat and decodeObject, decodeFloat.

How the data of the objects are encoded or decoded is the task of the coder object. NSCoder is an abstract class. Therefore we need a concrete subclass for the coder. There are three types of archives: sequential, keyed and distributed archives.

Sequential archives read and write data sequentially and you have to use the same order for reading and writing in your messages. Keyed archives use naming values, like property lists, and are accessible directly by the key. The last type is if you have distributed objects.

However, only the keyed archives are interesting for us, because sequential archives only exists in older versions of Mac OS X and are deprecated. If we have prepared our class with the NSCoding protocol, it is very simple to store and load this object to and from the user defaults.

The class-method archivedDataWithRootObject, shown in listing 4.7, is serializing the object *lastSavedLocation* and the result will be saved into a NSData instance. Now the new data object can be saved with the known messages.

```
NSData *data = [NSKeyedArchiver archivedDataWithRootObject:
                             self.model.lastSavedLocation];
[userdefaults setObject:data forKey:LASTSAVEDLOCATION];
[userdefaults synchronize];
```

Listing 4.7: Saving an object to UserDefaults

9

To load data from the user defaults into an object we need a NSKeyedUnarchvier to get the data with the class-method unarchiveObjectWithData.

```
NSData *data = [userDefaults objectForKey:LASTSAVEDLOCATION];
if (data)
{
    self.lastSavedLocation = [[mlvAnnotation alloc] init];
    self.lastSavedLocation = [NSKeyedUnarchiver
                              unarchiveObjectWithData:data];
}
```

Listing 4.8: Loading UserDefaults into an object

4.2 Documents

Property lists are an easy way to store data in your application and are generally used for user defaults and small data objects. If you want to save pictures, databases or other big documents you have to create a document and save that directly to the file system. This can be done in three different ways: UIDocument, Core Data or you can implement your own solution to write the data as file.

Mobile devices have special requirements of handling data, user operability and security. This results in some peculiarities how the file system and data of the applications are organized.

4.2.1 File System

As desktop user you have access to the file system with the Explorer or Finder and to manipulate the files directly, but this way to handle files is not possible on Apple's mobile devices, instead of the file handling is performed on the applications.

iOS is a UNIX-based operating system, just like OS X, so the file system is also a UNIX file system. The user does not have access to the file system. Each application has its own storage and cannot access to data from any other applications. This means the application is running in a sandbox, separated from all other applications. Apple describes this feature with "Every App Is an Island" [12] (File Management - File System Programming Guide - File System Basic). The application can only write to directories inside the sandbox. There are some exceptions for contacts or music. However, there is a way to open documents in other applications with a "Open in ..." functionality. This functionality is provided by the UIDocumentInteractionController class, with little lines of code.

Directory	Description
<ApplicationHome>/AppName.app	This directory includes the application.
<ApplicationHome>/Documents/	The user data should save into this directory.
<ApplicationHome>/Documents/Inbox	This directory is for any incoming data, like mail attachments.
<ApplicationHome>/Library/	Use this directory for any other data, which aren't user data.
<ApplicationHome>/tmp/	In this directory you can save any temporary files.

Table 4.2: iOS App Directories

The standard directories of an application looks like table 4.2. Normally, the user data of your application is stored in the Documents path. The foundation framework defines the constants NSDocumentDirectory and NSUserDomainMask to easily find out the user document directory.

As mentioned before, you don't have access to the file system, so you need the NSFileManager class to perform file operations. The class method defaultManager returns a shared file manager, which can be used for the most file operations. The location of the file can be described as string with NSString operations or as URL with URL operations. The URL class has a more efficient internal representation and you also can save bookmarks of URL.

The listing 4.9 gets the local user documents directory and saves an array of property list objects to a file using the message writeToURL. Also NSString, NSData and NSDictionary provides this method to write directly a file and it is not necessary to create a document object.

```
1  NSURL *docDir = [[[ NSFileManager defaultManager] URLsForDirectory:
       NSDocumentDirectory inDomains:NSUserDomainMask] lastObject];
   NSURL *file = [docDir URLByAppendingPathComponent:@"LastSavedLocation"];
3      [self.locations writeToURL:file atomically:YES];
```

Listing 4.9: Save an Array to File

The NSFileManager class is also needed for saving your own documents, which have to be a subclass of UIDocument, but also databases with the Core Date framework. Chapter 5 describes, how documents and databases can be stored to the iCloud with the usage of the NSFileManager.

With the help of the NSFileManager you easily can get an array of the files of a specified directory, for instance to show a list of files in a tableview window. Listing 4.10 shows how you can get this array of files either as strings or URLs. The URL method *contentsOfDirectoryAtURL:includingPropertiesForKeys:options:error* allows additional parameters to limit the search results, for instance to exclude hidden files.

```
1  -(NSArray *)listFileAtPath:(NSString *)path
   {
3      NSArray *directoryContent = [[NSFileManager defaultManager]
          contentsOfDirectoryAtPath:path
5          error:nil];
       return directoryContent;
7  }

9  -(NSArray *)listFileAtURL:(NSURL *)url
   {
11     NSArray *directoryContent = [[NSFileManager defaultManager]
          contentsOfDirectoryAtURL:url
13         includingPropertiesForKeys:[NSArray arrayWithObject:NSURLNameKey]
          options:NSDirectoryEnumerationSkipsHiddenFiles
15         error:nil];
       return directoryContent;
17 }
```

Listing 4.10: List Files of a Directory

4.2.2 UIDocument

Property lists are useful for instance for user settings, but have some limitations in memory size, object types or handling. Otherwise the user can create, read and write content, for example text or images, with your application. In that case it is better you create a document based application. A document is an instance of a UIDocument subclass and is part of the model in a MVC (Model - View - Controller) designed application, but you can also see the document as model controller for your data model.

UIDocument provide some features and behaviours, which facilitate the handling of reading and writing the data. This is happen which facilitate handling in the background. In most cases it isn't necessary to send a save message directly, because the framework does the saving automatic, like the user defaults. I UIDocument is also integrated in iCloud, so if the application also uses iCloud to store the documents into the iCloud, there isn't to change your code, only the location of the file or directory is different. In conjunction with iCloud it is possible, that a document could have a version conflict, the document was changed on two or more devices, before the synchronization was finished. A support for handling of this conflicts is also included.

To create a document in your application you need a subclass of UIDocument. This subclass includes the data of the document and two methods for reading and writing. You must override those methods. First one is the method loadFromContents:ofType:error:, which is loading the data of your document. The method contentsForType:error: returns a snapshot of the data to UIDocument, which can be saved as file.

There are two mechanisms to store the document on the file system with using of NSData or NSFileWrapper. Which one should be used is depending on the structure of the data in your data model in memory. With NSData the documents data is saved as flat file and is recommended for simple data objects such as text. If you have multiple data objects, for instance text and images, you should use NSFileWrapper, which saves those objects as separated files into an directory. This directory is your file package of your stored document. [12] (Data Management - Designing a Document-Based Application)

UIDocument with NSData

If you load and store your document with NSData, your data must be converted from your object types to NSData and vice versa. That means if you use your custom object types, have to implement the NSCoding protocol to serialize the data, as described in subsection 4.1.3 on page 9.

The class mlvDocumentData in listing 4.11 is the data model for the document. The model includes two properties (a text and an image) and implements the encode and decode methods of the NSCoding protocol to make sure that the documents data can be converted to NSData. As mentioned before the preferred way for loading / storing those data is NSFileWrapper, but that isn't mandatory.

```
@interface mlvDocument : UIDocument
@property (strong, nonatomic) mlvDocumentData *data;
@end
```

Listing 4.11: UIDocument Interface

The method contentsForType:error: (listing 4.12) gets the data and returns a snapshot as NSData.

```
1  -(id)contentsForType:(NSString *)typeName
                error:(NSError *__autoreleasing *)outError
3  {
       return [NSKeyedArchiver archivedDataWithRootObject:self.data];
5  }
```

Listing 4.12: UIDocument with NSData

To get the data of a stored document the method loadFromContents:ofType:error: is used (listing 4.13). The object contents includes the NSData representation of the data object, which is unarchieved to an instance of mlvDocument.

```
1  -(BOOL) loadFromContents:(id)contents
                    ofType:(NSString *)typeName
3                   error:(NSError *__autoreleasing *)outError
   {
5      if ( [contents length] > 0) {
           self.data = [NSKeyedUnarchiver unarchiveObjectWithData:contents];
7      } else {
           self.data = [[mlvDocumentData alloc] init];
9      }
       return YES;
11 }
```

Listing 4.13: UIDocument with NSData

UIDocument with NSFileWrapper

Instead of using NSData to store your data as single file, you also can use the methods of the NSFileWrapper class to create a file package. The data will be saved as separated files in the package. A file wrapper is file-system node, for instance a directory, a file or a symbolic link. In usage with the data of the object the file wrapper is a directory and includes the content as files. The data of our model mlvDocumentData will be saved as NSData representation into two separate files of package, one text and one image file.

Your document class needs a property or instance variable for the file wrapper and must also override the contentsForType:error: and loadFromContents:ofType:error:, such as seen by the NSData mechanism.

To store your data you have to create a file wrapper for the package and to add one more file wrapper for each data, which should be saved as separate file with the converted data. Listing 4.14 shows the neccessary parts of a working mechanism for one property.

At first you have to initialize the file wrapper, if it doesn't exists yet. The initialization methods for the container are *initDirectoryWithFileWrappers* and for the files *initRegularFile-WithContents*.

```
1  -(id)contentsForType:(NSString *)typeName
                error:(NSError *__autoreleasing *)outError
3  {
     // init self.fileWrapper ...
5
       NSDictionary *fileWrappers = [self.fileWrapper fileWrappers];
7      if (self.data.text != nil)
       {
9          [self.fileWrapper removeFileWrapper:[fileWrappers objectForKey:
               TEXTFILENAME]];
```

```
         NSData *textData = [self.data.text dataUsingEncoding:
            NSUTF8StringEncoding];
11       NSFileWrapper *textFileWrapper = [[NSFileWrapper alloc]
            initRegularFileWithContents:textData];
         [textFileWrapper setPreferredFilename:TEXTFILENAME];
13       [self.fileWrapper addFileWrapper:textFileWrapper];
      }
15
      // next data ...
17
      return self.fileWrapper;
19 }
```

Listing 4.14: UIDocument with NSFileWrapper

Then you remove an existing file wrapper from your package. This is normally done, when the user has edited the document and wants to save the changes. Nothing happens when this wrapper doesn't exist. Before you can add your file wrappers to the directory file wrapper you have to convert the data and set a preferred file name, see lines (9 - 12).

Loading data from a file package you have to get the file wrappers, which are stored as dictionary in the package, load the data for each file name and encodes the data into their property (listing 4.15).

```
1 -(BOOL) loadFromContents:(id)contents
                  ofType:(NSString *)typeName
3                  error:(NSError *__autoreleasing *)outError
   {
5      self.fileWrapper = (NSFileWrapper *)contents;
      NSDictionary *fileWrappers = [self.fileWrapper fileWrappers];
7
      self.data.text = [[NSString alloc] initWithData:[[fileWrappers
         objectForKey:TEXTFILENAME] regularFileContents] encoding:
         NSUTF8StringEncoding];
9
   // next data ...
11
      return YES;
13 }
```

Listing 4.15: UIDocument with NSFileWrapper

Working with UIDocument

The file handling with UIDocument in your application is equal no matter which method you choose. Each document has the following metadata to manage the file handling: File URL, Document name, a file type, the modification date and a document state. The file URL is mandatory to locate the file on the file system. If you create or open a file you have set a file URL. The default file name of the document is the last part of the URL, but it is also possible to set an other file name by overriding the getter method of *localizedName*. The file type identifies the type of the document based on the extension of the file URL. This extension has to match with a Uniform Type Identifier (UTI). A UTI is described in a reverse DNS format, for instance *com.myname.mylocationviewer.myfiletype*. If your document is used only in your iOS application a matching between extension and UTI isn't necessary. [12] (Data Management - Data Types & Collections - Uniform Type Identifiers Overview)

The data of the last modification is useful to handle version conflicts of your, especially in conjunction with the iCloud storage. When the user is manipulating the file by adding new content or editing the current content the document can have different states. Those states are shown in table 4.3. You should observe the document state in your application and do some reaction, for instance if a saving error occurs. An observer is simply added in the view controller of the document edit with the UIDocumentStateChangedNotification.

Document State	Description
UIDocumentStateNormal	Document is open, without any conflcts.
UIDocumentStateClosed	Document is closed, because it cannot be opened.
UIDocumentStateConflict	A version conflict exists (only by using iCloud).
UIDocumentStateSavingError	The Document cannot be saved.
UIDocumentStateEditingDisabled	Editing isn't safe at the moment.

Table 4.3: DocumentState

After initializing the document with the file URL - how to get the URL is described in section 4.2.1 - the user can manipulate the contents of the file. The method openWithCompletionHandler: opens the file asynchronously in the background and expect a block, which is running, when the completion is finished. In this block you can set the properties of the data model, if the opening was successful, otherwise some error handling.

```
[self.document openWithCompletionHandler:
^(BOOL success) {
    if (success) {
        NSLog(@"Opened");
        self.documentTextView.text = self.document.data.text;
        self.imageView.image = self.document.data.image;
    } else {
        NSLog(@"Not opened");
    }
}];
```

Listing 4.16: openWithCompletionHandler

The saving method saveToURL:forSaveOperation:completionHandler works at the same way, but needs two more parameters, the document URL for the location and an constant for the save operation. The save operation can be UIDocumentSaveForCreating or UIDocumentSaveForOverwriting.

```
[self.document saveToURL:self.documentURL
    forSaveOperation:UIDocumentSaveForOverwriting
    completionHandler:^(BOOL success) {
        if (success){
            NSLog(@"Saved for overwriting");
        } else {
            NSLog(@"Not saved for overwriting");
        }
    }];
```

Listing 4.17: saveToURL:forSaveOperation:completionHandler

A new document is created by initialzing an object of the document class and calling the saveToURL:forSaveOperation:completionHandler: with the constant UIDocumentSaveForCreating.

A simple way to debug what happens with the files in your application, is to use the iPhone Simulator and look with the Finder into the Documents directory ~/Library/Application Support/iPhone Simulator/[iOS-Version]/Applications/[appGUID]/Documents/. This directory shows the saved files as flat files or as directories with separate files, depending on the used storage method (NSData or NSFileWrapper).

UIDocument provides much more features, which you can use or adopt, for example auto saving, change tracking or incremental reading/writing. It is also possible to modify your subclass to add a document preview.

4.3 Database

Apple also supports database applications on mobile devices since the iOS version 3.0 with the Core Data framework. Core Data isn't a database, it does only abstract the access to persistent store and provides most of the needed features automaticly with a managed object context. There are three kinds of persistent stores: XML, SQLite and atomic (XML is not available in IOS). [12] (Core Data Programming Guide - Persistent Store Features)

The Core Data provides many features for instance change tracking, filtering or grouping data, relationship maintenance, and so on. In this paper I introduce the important parts of the Core Data framework, which are also necessery for implementing database applications with iCloud support.

4.3.1 SQLite

A traditional relational database system consits of the parts: a server, which stores the database and one or more clients with a user application, which connect to the database and manipulate the entries of the tables.

The SQLite database system works with an other concept, which is more useful for mobile devices. SQLite is a server-less database architecture (see figure 4.3) and must not be installed. It also does not need any configuration or an administrator account to run. The database is stored into a single file on the device.

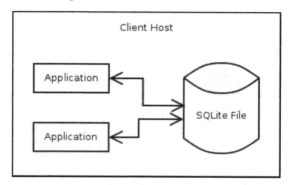

Figure 4.3: SQLite server-less architecture [13]

SQLite is designed for special usages and not to replace a big client/server databases like oracle. It works well in embedded devices, websites with low traffic or internal databases. In other situations, for instance large databases or if you need a high concurrency a RDBMS will be a better choice. [13]

However, this database engine is usable for almost all applications, so we don't need an extra database server and has implemented the most SQL standard syntax. In your iOS applications, normally you don't have to implement direct access to the SQLite database with SQL statements, instead use the Core Data framework to abstract the database layer.

4.3.2 Core Data

With the Core Data framework you can use your object oriented data model, instead of using SQL statements or XML syntax for storing data to the database. The Core Data framework abstracts the access to the data to a higher level, but supports many database features, including 1:n relationships.

Xcode helps you to design your entities of your data model and also generates the corresponding data classes. Nevertheless if you plan a big database application you should familiar with the Entity Relationship Model (ER-Model) for optimizing your data structure.

Organizing Data

Without the usage of the Core Data you have to structure in collections like lists or dictionaries manually (see figure 4.4), and also to implement the code for adding, deleting, fetching data objects.

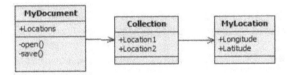

Figure 4.4: Data Collection Example

If you use the Core Data framework your data object type is similar, but the used classes and mechanisms a quite different. Figure 4.5 shows the same data structure if the usage of the Core Data classes.

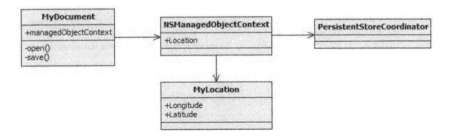

Figure 4.5: Core Data Example

Core Data Classes

The framework provides many classes, shown in table 4.4, which are necessary for building database applications. In Xcode you can create a new "Master-Detail Application" project with Core Data support and you will get a simple working database application. The AppDelegate class includes instances of the managed object context, managed object model and the persistent store coordinator. The master view controller includes methods for fetching and deleting data, but also including new data. However, you are able to implement your database application, based on that template.

Class Name	Usage
NSManagedObject	Generic class for your data class
NSManagedObjectContext	Actions, changes in your database
NSManagedObjectModel	Database schema, structure
NSPersistentStoreCoordinator	Persisting data
NSFetchRequest	Requesting data
NSPredicate	Specifying search queries
NSEntityDescription	Describes the entity

Table 4.4: Core Data Classes

Nevertheless I advise to not use this framework and create a new project without the Core Data support, because Apple provides with the iOS 5 SDK a new class, called UIManagedObject. UIManagedObject is a subclass of UIDocument and integrates all needed Core Data classes, In most cases you can use UIManagedObject directly and it isn't necessary to create a specific subclass.

The document handling (open, close, save, ...) works just like documents with a subclass of UIDocument. You only have to create an instance of UIManagedDocument and initialize it with the URL of the database. After initialzing your managed document has a managed object context and the persistent store coordinator. [12] (Data Management - UIManagedDocument Class Reference)

In this chapter I describe how to implement database applications using UIManagedDocument, because it is much easier to implement. This class also provides iCloud support.

Generating the Data Model

One of the first steps during creating a database application is to generate your data model. The data model can be generated in Xcode with an interactive editor. You can easily add new entities and setup the name and data types for the attributes. Further you can add some fetch requests for your entities. Figures 4.7 and 4.6 show the two views for a location entity.

Figure 4.6: LocationEntity

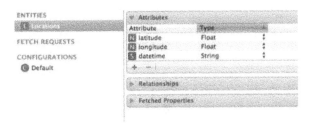

Figure 4.7: Entity Editor

After creating your entities you can use them in your application with the NSManagedObject class. NSManagedObject is a generic class for your data model and the access to the attributes is not as usual as the access to other objects.

You have to implement the access to the properties of your entity like the access to a property list with keys. Listing 4.18 creates a new managed object model (your data) with a NSEntityDescription object, which describes the entity of your data object or rather a row in a database table. With the class method *+ (id)insertNewObjectForEntityForName:(NSString *)entityName inManagedObjectContext:(NSManagedObjectContext *)context* you create a new entity for the specified managed object context. The managed object context represents your database. After creating the managed object, you can set the values of the attributes with *setValue:forKey:*. The last step is to call the save message of the managed object context to commit your changes.

```
NSManagedObject *newLocation =
    [NSEntityDescription
        insertNewObjectForEntityForName:@"Locations"
            inManagedObjectContext:self.locationDB.
                managedObjectContext];

[newLocation setValue:self.annotation.title forKey:@"datetime"];
[self.locationDB.managedObjectContext save:&error]
```

Listing 4.18: Insert a new Object into Database

This mechanism works fine, but it isn't very comfortable for the developer. It would be more beautiful to use the dot notation for the properties like any other objects. You can use the dot notation by subclassing the NSManagedObject class. Xcode provides the command "Create NSManagedObject Subclass..." in the "Editor" menu bar, but if you have some relationships between your entities, you have to start this command twice to generate the subclasses correctly. The result is a interface and implementation file for each entity and looks like listings 4.19 and 4.20 for the Locations entity.

```
@interface Locations : NSManagedObject
@property (nonatomic, retain) NSString * datetime;
@property (nonatomic) float latitude;
@property (nonatomic) float longitude;
@end
```

Listing 4.19: NSManagedObject Subclass Interface

```
1  @implementation Locations
   @dynamic datetime;
3  @dynamic latitude;
   @dynamic longitude;
5  @end
```

Listing 4.20: NSManagedObject Subclass Implementation

The interface file looks like you expected. The file includes each attribute of your entity as property. But the implementation file uses a new keyword: @dynamic instead of @synthesize. The @synthesize directive creates for your properties the getter and setter methods automatically in your class. Core Data creates the getter and setter dynamicly and there is no need to implement those methods in your class. Apple advises to use @dynamic, because Core Data generates the methods more efficiently than you can implement tehm. @dynamic tells the compiler that the getter and setter are somewhere else implemented and not in the class.

Now you can use the usual way for accessing the properties with the dot notation. The same function of listing 4.18 with subclassing the NSManagedObject class looks like listing 4.21

```
1      Locations *newLocation =
           (Locations *)[NSEntityDescription
3              insertNewObjectForEntityForName:@"Locations"
                   inManagedObjectContext:self.locationDB.
                       managedObjectContext];
5
       newLocation.datetime = self.annotation.title;
7      [self.locationDB.managedObjectContext save:&error];
```

Listing 4.21: Insert a new Object into Database

Deleting a object from a table works straightforward. You only have to call the deleteObject method of managed object context, see listing 4.22. The deleting will be performed, when you send the save method of the context.

```
1  Locations *location = [self.fetchedResultsController
                       objectAtIndexPath:indexPath];
3  [self.fetchedResultsController.managedObjectContext
                       deleteObject:location];
```

Listing 4.22: Delete an Object from Database

Fetching Data

Now you can add and delete objects to/from your database, but your application also needs also a view to present the data. This presentation can be done in different ways, for instance in a table view. But it is also possible to present your data in a map view.

No matter how the data is represented, you need a fetch request to get the data from the managed object context. At first you create an instance of NSFetchRequest and then you can specify some predicates or set the sortDescriptor to modify the fetch result.[12] (Core Data Programming Guide - Fetching Managed Objects)

To fetch your request you need the NSFetchedResultsController class, which to manage the results and also to configure the cells in a table view with the data. Listing 4.23 show a simple fetch request from the Locations table sorting by the datetime attribute. After the setup of the fetchedResultsController you have to call the performFetch method to get the fetch result.

```
- (void)setupFetchedResultsController
{
    NSFetchRequest *request = [NSFetchRequest fetchRequestWithEntityName:@"
        Locations"];

    NSSortDescriptor *sort = [NSSortDescriptor sortDescriptorWithKey:@"
        datetime"
        ascending:YES
        selector:@selector(localizedCaseInsensitiveCompare:)];

    request.sortDescriptors = [NSArray arrayWithObject:sort];

    self.fetchedResultsController = [[NSFetchedResultsController alloc]
        initWithFetchRequest:request
        managedObjectContext:self.locationDB.managedObjectContext
        sectionNameKeyPath:nil
        cacheName:nil];
}
```

Listing 4.23: Setup a FetchedResultsController

The NSFetchedResultsController class provides the data for an easy use in an UITableView. You can easily set the number of rows in a section and also set the data for a specific row, shown in listing 4.24.

```
- (UITableViewCell *)tableView:(UITableView *)tableView
    cellForRowAtIndexPath:(NSIndexPath *)indexPath
{
    // ... configure your cell ...

    Locations *location = [self.fetchedResultsController
            objectAtIndexPath:indexPath];
    cell.textLabel.text = location.datetime;

    return cell;
}
```

Listing 4.24: Set Data for a Cell

A database application with an UITableView is a usual and often used way to represent the data, so the Stanford University provides a subclass of the UITableViewController, which includes the NSFetchedResultsControllerDelegate.

The class CoreDataTableViewController [14] (Lection 14: Core Data Demo - CoreDataTableViewController.zip) has the typical standard implemention for the data source and helps you to debug your fetch requests. If your table view controller is a subclass of CoreDataTableViewController, for the data source you only have to implement the method tableView:cellForRowAtIndexPath: as shown in listing 4.24, but also of course the document handling and your own functionality.

Another way to visualize the data in your application is for instance a map view if you have location data. The fetched results controller provides a method to get the result as an array, but in this case you don't this controller. You also can execute a fetch directly from the managed object context with the method executeFetchRequest:error:.

If the objects of this array includes location data it is possible to create annotations, which you can add to the map view. The method loadAnnotations in listing 4.25 shows how you can implement that.

```
 1   - (void) loadAnnotations
 2   {
 3       NSFetchRequest *request = [NSFetchRequest
 4           fetchRequestWithEntityName:@"Locations"];
 5
 6       NSArray *result = [self.locationDB.managedObjectContext
 7           executeFetchRequest:request error:nil];
 8
 9       for (Locations *loc in result)
10       {
11           CLLocationCoordinate coord;
12           coord = CLLocationCoordinate2DMake(loc.latitude, loc.longitude);
13           mlvAnnotation *annotation = [[mlvAnnotation alloc]
14               initWithTitle:loc.datetime
15                   andCoordinate:coord];
16           [self.annotations addObject:annotation];
17       }
18
19       [self.mapView addAnnotations:self.annotations];
20   }
```

Listing 4.25: Load Annotations from Database

Now the user can see and modify the data of your database application. However the Core Data frameworks provides much more features, for instance property validations, filtering with NSPredicate, relationships, which you can use if you need for your application. Core Data also provides an efficient iCloud support. The next chapter describes how you can extend your database application for iCloud usage.

5 Saving data in the iCloud

The previous chapter described three different mechanisms for storing local data. Which one of them is useful is depending on the type of data. However, nowadays many users don't use only one device. They have two or more devices, for instance an iPhone and an iPad or even perhaps a MacBook. The requirements of those users are to have the data on all devices. A solution for those requirements is the iCloud.

iCloud also allows three mechanisms to store the data in the cloud: Key-Value storage, Document storage and Core Data Storage. Those cloud mechanisms correspond to the local mechanisms. The Key-Value storage can save property lists and user default values, the document storage stores documents using the NSFileManager class and databases are saved in the Core Data Storage. Apple provides two APIs for the iCloud storage, one for the Key-Value storage and one for the Document storage, because the Core Data storage is a subset of the Document storage. The table 5.1 shows the differences between those two kinds of iCloud storage. [12] (iCloud Design Guide - iCloud Fundamentals)

Attribute	Key-Value storage	Document storage
Purpose	User documents, complex data	Preferences, configurations
Data Format	File & Packages	Property Lists
Capacity	iCloud space of the user	1 MB per app
Managing Data	NSFileManager	NSUbiquitousKeyValueStore
Locating Data	NSMetaDataQuery	NSUbiquitousKeyValueStore

Table 5.1: iCloud Storages

Figure 5.1 shows a schematic overview of the different storages of an application. The local data are stored in the sandbox container and the iCloud data in the Ubiquity container. The ubiquity container is the local copy of the iCloud storage and is outside of the application sandbox. The reason, why this container is outside the sandbox, is it possible to share this data not only on different devices, but also on various applications. [12] (iCloud Design Guide - iCloud Fundamentals).

The iCloud storage has many advantages and useful features for the user, but it isn't a good idea to save all your data into the cloud, because the Key-Value storage and the Document storage are limited. Temporary files, caching files, generated data, which can be recreated by your application and database should save into the local storage. The API of the Database storage provides a mechanism to avoid saving the whole database file.

5.1 Key-Value Storage

Property Lists save data as keys and values in the application local storage of the device. If you want to save this kind of data in the iCloud you can use the Key-Value storage. This storage works similar as the user defaults with the NSUserDefaults class. The big difference is the Key-Value storage is available on all devices, which are iCloud enabled for that application. You can use this storage for saving user settings, default values, configuration settings or any

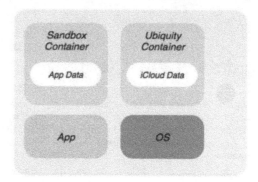

Figure 5.1: Application Storage [12] (iCloud Design Guide - iCloud Fundamentals)

other small data. Another usage of that storage is to save the state of the application, so that the user can continue his work or game on the second device at the same position. Data, which is necessary for your application - for instance the setting if iCloud is enabled or not - should not be saved to the iCloud storage, because your device possibly can't have an access to the iCloud. In that case it is better to save this data in the user default storage and additionally for the synchronization into the Key-Value storage. Passwords also should not be saved to the Key-Value storage. Apple provides keychain services with a secure storage for passwords and keys [12] (Security - Keychain Services Programming Guide). It isn't mandatory that the user has an iCloud from the beginning, your application can also use the Key-Value storage. The data will be uploaded to the iCloud, as soon as the user has created an iCloud account.

The maximum size of the Key-Value storage is only 1 megabyte and not more than 1024 keys. The key string has a maximum length of 64 byte as UTF-8 character set. If you need more memory, you must use the the document storage and save your data as file or database. [12] (iCloud Design Guide - Designing Key-Value Data in iCloud)

To use the Key-Value storage you have to setup the entitlements for iCloud and this storage in your target in Xcode. The class method defaultStore of the class NSUbiquitousKeyValueStore returns a object with the shared iCloud key-value storage (compare with standardUserDefaults in NSUserDefaults).

Loading (see listing 5.1) and saving (listing 5.2) data from and to iCloud is as easy as from user defaults with just a few lines of code:

```
- (NSData *)loadLastSavedLocationFromICloud
{
    NSData *data = nil;
    NSUbiquitousKeyValueStore *iCloudUserDefaults =
        [NSUbiquitousKeyValueStore defaultStore];
    data = [iCloudUserDefaults objectForKey:LASTSAVEDLOCATION];
    return data;
}
```

Listing 5.1: Load Key-Value Data

Changed values will be saved to the file system periodically by the operating system. To force the saving of the changed values you can send the synchronize message. The data will be written immediately, but this doesn't mean that the data is uploaded to the iCloud now.

iCloud is only notified there are changed values. You cannot affect when data is uploaded, iOS uploads the data several times per minute to the Key-Value storage.

```
- (void)saveLastLocationToICloud:(NSData *)data
{
    NSUbiquitousKeyValueStore *iCloudUserDefaults = [
        NSUbiquitousKeyValueStore defaultStore];
    [iCloudUserDefaults setObject:data forKey:LASTSAVEDLOCATION];
    [iCloudUserDefaults synchronize];
}
```

Listing 5.2: Save Key-Value Data

If you compare those listings with the listings for loading/saving user defaults, you will see that there are the same messages (for instance setObject forKey or objectForKey) used. The difference is the NSUbiquitousKeyValueStore instead of NSUserDefaults.

This concept can be exploited to abstract the storage (iCloud or local) from the loading and saving methods and make it more generic, shown in listing 5.3 and 5.4.

```
- (NSData *)loadLastLocationFromStorage:(id)storage
{
    NSData *data = nil;
    if ([storage isKindOfClass:[NSUserDefaults class]] ||
        [storage isKindOfClass:[NSUbiquitousKeyValueStore class]])
    {
        data = [storage objectForKey:LASTSAVEDLOCATION];
    }
    return data;
}
```

Listing 5.3: Generic Load Method

```
- (void)saveLastLocation:(NSData *)data toStorage:(id)storage
{
    if ([storage isKindOfClass:[NSUserDefaults class]] ||
        [storage isKindOfClass:[NSUbiquitousKeyValueStore class]])
    {
        [storage setObject:data forKey:LASTSAVEDLOCATION];
        [storage synchronize];
    }
}
```

Listing 5.4: Generic Save Method

Use this generic methods by adding the right parameter of the storage. This might be useful if you have an application setting of 'iCloud enabled' in the user defaults and you want avoid asking which storage is enabled. After initializing the application the used storage is saved into a property or instance variable.

Listing 5.5 shows an example usage for saving the data to iCloud.

```
self.storage = [NSUbiquitousKeyValueStore defaultStore];
[self saveLastLocation:data
            toStorage:self.storage];
```

Listing 5.5: Save To Storage

5.2 Document Storage

With the Document storage your application can save the user documents in the iCloud, which are available on all other devices. The document storage is not within the sandbox container, but in an extra ubiquity container. You have to set the entitlement for this container in your Xcode project for your application. Before you can use this container call the method *(NSURL *)URLForUbiquityContainerIdentifier:(NSString *)containerID* in your AppDelegate class. If you set the containerID to nil you will get the first ubiquity container of your entitlements. These entitlements are useful, because your application have access to ubiquity containers of other applications if allowed.

After setup the ubiquity container the application can read or write documents, which will be synchronized with iCloud with using the already known mechanisms and classes NSFileManager and UIDocument. In section 4.2.2 I have described the way to implement your own local documents in an application. This way is exactly the same for using with iCloud. The only difference is the URL of the directory.

A simple solution to get the document URL in your application, depending on if the user has enabled iCloud for this application, is shown in listing 5.6). If iCloud usage is enabled, get the URL with URLForUbiquityContainerIdentifier, otherwise URLsForDirectory.

```
1   if (self.iCloudUsed)
        directoryURL =[[[NSFileManager defaultManager]
3                        URLForUbiquityContainerIdentifier:@"VGD52CBBYU.
                         cc.bachmaier.myLocationViewer"]
                       URLByAppendingPathComponent:@"Documents"];
5   else
        directoryURL = [[[NSFileManager defaultManager] URLsForDirectory:
            NSDocumentDirectory inDomains:NSUserDomainMask] lastObject];
```

Listing 5.6: Getting Document URL

In iOS the documents are not downloaded automatically to your device. The download will be started only, when you open the file with openWithCompletionHandler or you explicitly start the download with *[[NSFileManager defaultManager] startDownloadingUbiquitousItemAtURL:fileURL error:&error];* The operating system handles the serialization of the user documents and the transfer from and to the iCloud in the background using the file coordinator and file presenter. Both those classes are needed for an safe reading and writing the data.

The UIDocument class automatically uses the file coordinator and file presenter. On the first upload of a document in the ubiquity container to the iCloud the complete file including the metadata is transmitted, the same on the first download. After that, only the metadata and the changed bits of the document will be transmitted to reduce network traffic and the power consumption of the mobile device. [12] (iCloud Storage - Using iCloud Document Storage)

However, there are no changes in your code by adding the iCloud support in your application, but you have to be aware, that multiple and simultaneous accesses to the directories and files are possible. This may result in a conflict of the user documents, which you have to handle. Otherwise it would be a nice feature if you have a table view with the documents and this view will be updated if there any changes, for example a new document was added on an other device.

5.2.1 Update Notification

You can get updates of changes in your Document storage by using the NSMetaDataQuery class. The metadata of the files (filename, modification data, size, file type) are automatly downloaded to device, so you can check if there are any changes.

```
_query = [[NSMetadataQuery alloc] init];
[_query setSearchScopes:[NSArray arrayWithObjects:
    NSMetadataQueryUbiquitousDocumentsScope, nil]];
[_query setPredicate:[NSPredicate predicateWithFormat:@"%K LIKE '*'",
    NSMetadataItemFSNameKey]];
```
Listing 5.7: MetaData Query URL

Instead of getting a file list with the file manager, use a metadata query and notification as in listing 5.7. The query result is an array with the meta data of the matching files, either the file is downloaded or not.

You have to set an observer to get a notification if the gathering of the metadata is finished (NSMetadataQueryDidFinishGatheringNotification) and usefully a second observer to get a notification for any update (NSMetadataQueryDidUpdateNotification).

```
[notificationCenter addObserver:self
    selector:@selector(fileListReceived)
    name:NSMetadataQueryDidFinishGatheringNotification
    object:_query];
```
Listing 5.8: NSMetadataQueryDidFinishGatheringNotification

The method fileListReceived (listing 5.8) is called after the metadata query notifications. In this method you can get the query results and reload your table view data for instance.

5.2.2 Conflict Handling

By adding iCloud support in your application it is possible to edit and save the document at the same time on different devices. This can result in a version conflict, for instance one device cannot upload the document to the iCloud. The system doesn't know, which version should be saved. You have to resolve those conflicts in your application. UIDocument provides a way to get an notification, when a change of the document state occurs. You have to add an observer for the UIDocumentStateChangedNotification.

How to resolve the conflict is up to you, depending on your requirements, for instance you can use the document with the latest modification date or you let the user choose which version should be saved. A third, but more difficult solution, is to merge the changes from both documents.The class NSFileVersion includes the necessary methods for resolving those conflicts. [12] (Data Management - NSFileVersion Class Reference)

5.3 Core Data Storage

Whereas the Document Storage is used for file based applications like documents or drawings the Core Data Storage provides database applications with iCloud support. The Core Data Storage isn't a seperate storage, but it is a part of the Document Storage and uses the same API.

The Core Data framework allows to use various file types for your database file, for instance SQLite, XML (not on iOS) or binary. But if you want to support iCloud in your database application, you should use the SQLite format to minimize the network traffic. SQLite allows incremental updates of the database to the iCloud Core Data Storage. If you use the binary store, the whole database must be uploaded to iCloud, but also downloaded to all connected devices. By using SQLite only the change log files are transmitted to and from iCloud. The local database will be updated with the received change logs. [12] (iCloud Design Guide - Designing for Core Data in iCloud)

The implementation of a database application with iCloud support is exactly the same as described in the previous chapter. You only have to set the URL of your managed document (the database file) to the ubiquity container, but outside the Documents directory, see listing 5.9 to implement the initializing for URL, depending on iCloud is enabled or not. Only with changing the URL your database applications includes iCloud support.

```
if (self.model.iCloud)
    url = [[NSFileManager defaultManager]
        URLForUbiquityContainerIdentifier:
            @"VGD52CBBYU.cc.bachmaier.myLocationViewer"];
else
    url = [[[NSFileManager defaultManager]
        URLsForDirectory:NSDocumentDirectory
        inDomains:NSUserDomainMask] lastObject];
```

Listing 5.9: Getting Managed Document URL

Now if the user changes the data on one device and starts the application on other devices with the same iCloud account, the change log files are downloaded and the application shows the updated data.

5.3.1 Update Notification

The Core Date framework also provides a notification when updates of the data are downloaded from iCloud. You can register this notification, like in listing 5.10, in your table view to reload the data. The object of the notification is your persistent store coordinator.

```
[[NSNotificationCenter defaultCenter]
    addObserver:self
    selector:@selector(documentContentsChanged:)
    name:NSPersistentStoreDidImportUbiquitousContentChangesNotification
    object:self.locationDB.managedObjectContext.
        persistentStoreCoordinator];
```

Listing 5.10: NSPersistentStoreDidImportUbiquitousContentChangesNotification

If any changes are downloaded from iCloud the method documentContentsChanged is called. In this method you have to merge the changes of your managed document and reload the table view. By using the CoreDataTableViewController class (see section 4.3.2) the method looks like listing 5.11. You don't have to call performFetch method again, because the observation of the fetched result controller is done by the delegation.

```
- (void)documentContentsChanged:(NSNotification *)notification
{
    [self.locationDatabase.managedObjectContext
        mergeChangesFromContextDidSaveNotification:notification];
}
```

Listing 5.11: documentContentsChanged

5.3.2 Conflict Handling

The big advantage of the Core Data storage or a Document story is the more intelligent data merging. If there exists two versions of a document on different devices, the iCloud can only mark this document has a conflict and it is up to you to resolve that.

However, if the user doesn't edit the same entities on different devices, Core Data is able to merge these changes of both devices. The framework allows various merge policies, the default policy is *NSErrorMergePolicy*. The *NSErrorMergePolicy* raises an error if there exist a version conflict and you have to implement your own conflict handling in the application.

Another way is to use *NSMergeByPropertyStoreTrumpMergePolicyType*, which gives the external changes the priority and this resolves the conflict automatically. [12] (Core Data - NSMergePolicy Class Reference)

Policy Type	Merging Policy
NSErrorMergePolicyType	Saving fails, if there is a conflict.
NSMergeByPropertyStoreTrumpMergePolicyType	External changes have the priority.
NSMergeByPropertyObjectTrumpMergePolicyType	In-memory changes have the priority.
NSOverwriteMergePolicyType	The persistent store will be overwritten.
NSRollbackMergePolicyType	The changes will be discarded.

Table 5.2: NSMergePolicyType

6 Summary

iCloud is Apple's cloud solution, which is fully integrated into mobile devices with iOS 5 and higher and has more than 100 milion users.Many successful applications integrates iCloud support, because this is expected by the users. In my paper I have described how you can extend your application with iCloud support.

There are three kinds of local data storage on iOS devices, depending on the type of data you want to save. Simple user settings, configuration values stored as property list or user defaults. Property lists have a limited space and are only for small data. Text files, images or other documents are stored as UIDocument and databases as UIManagedDocument. Chapter 4 described the implementation of each of the local storages.

For each of those types exist a corresponding iCloud storage type: Key-Value Storage for property lists, Document Storage for documents and Core Data Storage for databases.

For user defaults lists you have to use NSUbiquitousKeyValueStore instead of NSUserDefaults, but the handling is smilar and the conflict management is very simple - the last modification wins. Moreover, it is also very simple to transfer the key-values between the storages.

The handling with Documents and databases is also very easy, because it will be used the same classes. The only different is the URL of the files. Local files are located in the sandbox of the application, but iCloud files are stored in an ubiquity container. If you use iCloud for documents you only have to think about changing notifications and conflict handling. The necessary changes in your application is described in chapter 5.

Due to the many iCloud users you should extend your application with iCloud support and let the user the choice to use iCloud or not. The iOS SDK with the Foundation and Core Data frameworks helps you to implement the iCloud support, because there are not so many changes to do in your application by using the provided mechanisms.

Bibliography

[1] Microsoft, "Azure," online, 2012, http://www.windowsazure.com [Accessed: Nov 04, 2012].

[2] ——, "SkyDrive," online, 2012, http://www.skydrive.live.com [Accessed: Nov 04, 2012].

[3] Google, "Google Drive," online, 2012, http://www.drive.google.com [Accessed: Nov 04, 2012].

[4] Ubuntu, "Ubuntu One," online, 2012, http://www.one.ubuntu.com [Accessed: Nov 04, 2012].

[5] Apple, "iCloud Features," online, 2012, http://www.apple.com/icloud/features/ [Accessed: Nov 03, 2012].

[6] J. R. J.W. Rittinghouse, *Cloud Computing, Implementation, Management, and Security*. Taylor and Francis Group, 2010.

[7] T. G. P. Mell, "The NIST Definition of Cloud Computing," online, 2011, http://csrc.nist.gov/publications/nistpubs/800-145/SP800-145.pdf [Accessed: Nov 09, 2012].

[8] R. B. Qi Zhang, Lu Cheng, "Cloud computing: state-of-the-art and research challenges," online, 2010, http://cloud.pubs.dbs.uni-leipzig.de/sites/cloud.pubs.dbs.uni-leipzig.de/files/fulltext.pdf [Accessed: Nov 09, 2012].

[9] Apple, "iCloud," online, 2012, http://www.icloud.com [Accessed: Nov 03, 2012].

[10] ——, "iCloud Developer," online, 2012, https://developer.icloud.com [Accessed: Dec 03, 2012].

[11] F. Lardinois, "Apple Now Has 150 Million iCloud Users ," online, TechBrunch, 2010, http://techcrunch.com/2012/07/24/apple-q3-2012-icloud-users/ [Accessed: Dec 22, 2012].

[12] Apple, "iOS Developer Library," online, 2012, https://developer.apple.com/library/ios/navigation/ [Accessed: Nov 26, 2012].

[13] J.A.Kreibich, *Using SQLite*. O'Reilly, 2010.

[14] P. Hegarty, "CS193P iPhone Application Development," online, 2012, http://www.stanford.edu/class/cs193p/cgi-bin/drupal/downloads-2011-fall [Accessed: Jan 05, 2013].

List of Figures

List of Tables

List of Listings

List of Abbreviations

API	Application Programming Interface
IaaS	Infrastructure as a Service
MVC	Model View Controller
PaaS	Platform as a Service
plist	Property List
SaaS	Software as a Service
SDK	Software Development Kit
URL	Uniform Resource Locator
UTI	Uniform Type Identifier